The History of
The African & Caribbean Communities in Britain

Hakim Adi

Wayland

Titles in the History of Communities Series

The History of the African and Caribbean
   Communities in Britain

The History of the Asian Community
   in Britain

First published in 1995 by Wayland Publishers Ltd
61 Western Road, Hove, East Sussex, BN3 1JD,
England

© Copyright 1995 Wayland Publishers Ltd

Editor: Cath Senker
Designer: Jean Wheeler
Picture researcher: Shelley Noronha
Production controller: Carol Stevens

British Library Cataloguing in Publication Data
Adi, Hakim
The History of the African and Caribbean
Communities in Britain
I. Title II. Series
305.896041

ISBN 0-7502-1517-8

Printed and bound in Italy by G. Canale &
C.S.p.A., Turin

The author would like to thank the following for
their help in producing this book: Stephen
Bourne, George Matthews, Philip Vasili, Howard
Bloch, Marika Sherwood, Marij van Helmond and
Josephine Florent.

Notes on sources
1 P. Fryer, *Staying Power – The History of Black People in
Britain* (Pluto, 1984) pp.95-6
2. The *Gentleman's Magazine*, vol. 34, p.426, quoted
in A *History of the Black Presence in London* (Greater
London Council, 1986), p.25
3. The *London Packet* 27-29 August 1773, quoted in
P. Fryer, *Staying Power, op. cit.*, p.70.

Cover pictures: A Black family today (main
picture); West African seamen aboard the *Borrabool*
in about 1935.
Title page: Black coach boy in Clwyd, 19th century.
Contents page: Esther Bruce (1912–92) as a child.
She told her own life history in *The Sun Shone on
Our Side of the Street – Aunt Esther's Story* by
S. Bourne & E. Bruce.

Picture acknowledgements
The author and publishers would like to thank the following for allowing their illustrations to be reproduced in this book: Hakim Adi
40 (below); BBC Photo Library & Archive 40 (above); Bob Goodwin Archives 31; Bodleian Library 29; Stephen Bourne *contents page*, 38
(below); Bridgeman 5 (above), 18; British Library 11, 17, 21, 27; British Museum 12 (below); Chapel Studies (Z. Mukhida) 44; College
of Arms 6; Communist Party Picture Library 36; Eye Ubiquitous *cover* (main); Josephine Florent 4, 7; Fotomas Index 13, 19; Hulton
22, 28 (both), 37 (both), 38 (above), 41 (below), 42 (below), 43; Imperial War Museum 39; John Frost Historical Pictures 42 (above);
Johnston Trust 12 (above); Local Studies Library, London Borough of Newham 25; Mary Evans Picture Library 14, 15, 20, 23 (both);
National Museums & Galleries on Merseyside (R. Costello) 8, (Barbados Museum & Historical Society) 10 (above),
(R. Costello) 24; Museum in Docklands, PLA Collection *cover* (inset), 34; Museum of Antiquities of the University & the Society of
Antiquaries of Newcastle upon Tyne 5 (below); National Trust *title page*; Peter Newark 16; Royal Collection Enterprises 10 (below);
Scottish National Portrait Gallery 9 (above); Topham 9 (below), 30; The Voice Communications Group Ltd 33; Wandsworth Borough
Council 25 (above); Wayland 26; Welsh Industrial and Maritime Museum 25 (below), 41 (above); Western Mail and Echo
Ltd /Butetown History and Art Centre 32. Artwork on page 8 by Peter Bull.

Contents

1 The first Africans in Britain

Today there are hundreds of thousands of people in Britain who have migrated from Africa and the Caribbean. They and their children and grandchildren, who were born in Britain, are British citizens, but are still sometimes treated as if they are unwelcome foreigners. People who are of African and Caribbean origin are often called Black people. Today there are many Black people living in towns and cities throughout Britain. In some areas, where there are large numbers of Black people, distinct communities have been formed, although these have never been totally separate from the wider British population.

Many people think that Britain's Black population has only developed in modern times, especially since the end of the Second World War in 1945. In fact there have been African communities in some of Britain's major cities, such as London, for over 400 years. The first Africans may have come to Britain thousands of years ago, even before the ancestors of the English.

The Florent family in the early 1920s. Napoleon Florent (father) who was an actor, arrived from St Lucia in the Caribbean in 1907. Vivian Florent, the youngest child in the photo, lost his life in the Second World War.

This book will help you find out more about the history of African and Caribbean people in Britain. It is a history which is still often ignored even in schools. But without the contributions of the peoples of Africa and the Caribbean, Britain would never have become a wealthy country nor a major world power.

Africans in Britain

It is not yet clear when the first Africans arrived in Britain. Some of the first humans to reach Britain from what is today Spain, may have originally come from north Africa. Ancient folk tales tell of African people invading Britain thousands of years ago, even before the Roman conquest of AD 43. In these folk tales Africans were thought to be the builders of Stonehenge and other ancient stone circles.

Septimus Severus and his family, third century BC.

During Roman times African soldiers were stationed in Britain for many years. The Roman emperor Septimus Severus, who came from Libya, visited Britain and died in York in AD 211.

There are many other references to Africans and Black people in the early histories of Britain. Some tell of Africans invading Britain at the same time as the Angles and Saxons in the fifth century. In the Middle Ages, Africans were usually referred to as 'Blackamoors' or 'Moors', the name given to the north African conquerors of Spain from 711 to 1492.

This is the tombstone of Victor, a Black soldier in Roman Britain, described as a 'Moorish tribesman'. He died at South Shields, Tyneside aged twenty.

There are more reliable records from the early sixteenth century showing that African men, women and children lived in a number of towns in Scotland and England. The records do not show how many Africans lived in Britain at this time, nor where they came from. African servants, male and female, were employed at the court of the Scottish King James IV in 1505, and seem to have been well treated and well paid.

An African trumpeter was employed at the court of King Henry VII in 1507, and can be seen in this picture of the Westminster Tournament in 1511.

Africans in Elizabethan England

By the late sixteenth century there may have been hundreds of Africans in England, especially in London, but there are also records of African men and women living in towns such as Barnstaple and Plymouth. English ships sailed as far as the kingdom of Benin in West Africa, and English merchants traded with a number of other West African kingdoms. In 1555, five Africans from what is now Ghana visited England to be trained as interpreters for London merchants. Some Africans were employed as servants and entertainers, and there were African musicians and dancers at the court of Elizabeth I. During her reign (1558–1603), England began to participate in the transatlantic slave trade. From 1570 onwards some African slaves were brought to Britain as household servants.

But in 1596, Queen Elizabeth ordered the arrest of Africans in London, and some other towns, and their expulsion from England. They were to be exchanged for English prisoners in Spain and Portugal. In 1601 the queen issued a further order for the arrest and expulsion of Africans. This was the first time that Africans were singled out for such treatment in Britain. The queen's order showed that she believed that there were too many Africans in Britain, and that they were taking jobs and food away from English people at a time of famine and unemployment.

Paul Robeson playing Othello in Stratford-on-Avon in 1959.

It is interesting that William Shakespeare wrote his famous play *Othello* a few years after these expulsions. Shakespeare made the African, or Moorish general Othello the hero of this play, and describes him as brave and noble. In *The Merchant of Venice* Shakespeare portrays the Prince of Morocco in the same way. Despite Elizabeth I's attempts to expel some Africans, it seems unlikely that racism against Africans was widespread at this time, and England had important diplomatic ties with Morocco in north Africa. Some historians believe that Shakespeare himself was at one time in love with an African woman known as Lucy Morgan, who lived in London, and that he wrote of her beauty in one of his famous sonnets.

2
The 18th century:
slaves and free Africans

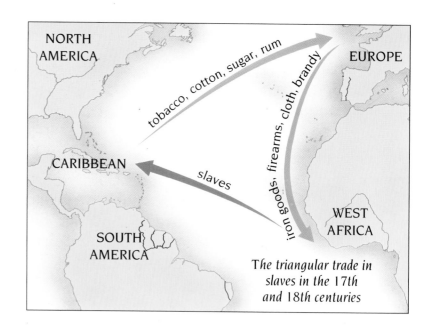

The triangular trade in slaves in the 17th and 18th centuries

The slave trade

Throughout the seventeenth century Britain's African population continued to grow, particularly after about 1650. At this time Britain became heavily involved in the African slave trade. British slave ship owners took Africans from West Africa and sold them as slaves in America and the Caribbean. Also, thousands of Africans were brought to Britain as slaves and servants, both from Africa and from England's new colonies in the Caribbean. The laws of England regarded African slaves as the property of their owners. African slaves were advertised for sale and sold openly at auctions in slave ports such as London, Bristol and Liverpool.

By the early eighteenth century Africans lived and worked in towns all over the country. The total African population may have been as large as 20,000. Most lived in London, but also in other cities. There may have been at least 5,000 Africans in Bristol at this time. It became the fashion for wealthy people to buy African boys as

Gallons of Water in a Minute, into a ¼ Inch and half Bore, from a Well 12 Feet deep, and 13 Feet from the Surface of the Water.

To be Sold, to the Highest Bidder,
At GEORGE's COFFEE-HOUSE, on Tuesday next, precisely at One o'Clock,

A NEGRO GIRL,

About Eight Years of Age, hath been from the Coast some Time, and is very healthy.

☞ The Proprietor of the said Girl having declin'd going to Sea, and being now settled in Worcestershire, would be glad to sell her on very reasonable Terms.

BARTLETT HODGETTS,
HABERDASHER, direct opposite GEORGE's COFFEE-

An advertisement for the sale of a Black girl in Williamson's Liverpool Advertiser, *about 1770.*

pages, often giving them to their children. Some were even made to wear brass or silver collars, given names such as Scipio and Pompey, and treated as if they were pets. Britain's royal family, aristocracy and first prime minister, Sir Robert Walpole (1676–1745) all owned slaves.

The slave trade helped to make Britain, the leading slave trader, one of the wealthiest countries in the world. Rich people in Britain made money from their ownership of plantations in the Caribbean, which produced tropical goods like sugar that were grown by African slaves. Wealthy people used money they earned from the slave trade to develop new industries such as shipbuilding, textiles and steel. The modern banks grew out of the wealth produced by the trade in slaves. By the 1770s British ships were transporting as many as 47,000 Africans to America and the Caribbean as slaves each year.

James Drummond, second Duke of Perth, with his slave.

A model of a slave ship showing how Africans were crammed in to be transported.

William Ansah, a prince from what is now Ghana, was sold into slavery. When he was freed he came to Britain.

Some Africans were employed as musicians in the British Army. This picture from about 1750 shows a trumpeter of the Horse Guards.

Free Africans

Some Africans came to Britain as free seamen or as representatives of African kings. In the eighteenth century wealthy and powerful African rulers sometimes sent their children to be educated or to trade. Philip Quaque, son of a king from what is now Ghana, was sent to school in England at the age of thirteen in 1754. In 1765 he became the first African to be ordained as a priest in the Church of England. He returned to West Africa as a missionary with a salary of £50 a year.

However, most of those who arrived were slaves. They wished to be free and many ran away from their owners. Seventeenth- and eighteenth-century newspapers often contained advertisements offering rewards for the return of runaway slaves. Some of these Africans were as young as eight years old.

Africans might be found doing many different types of jobs. Many were household servants, but some were agricultural workers or craftspeople. Others were musicians or entertainers like those who appeared in the Lord Mayor of London's annual procession from the early seventeenth century.

Owners sometimes educated their slaves, but even those who escaped must have found it difficult to find work. In 1731 the Lord Mayor of London banned Black people from taking up apprenticeships and so excluded them from learning a trade. A few Africans were able to earn wages and maintain their freedom, but many were forced to become beggars.

Ukawsaw Gronniosaw

We know something of the difficulties faced by poor Africans from the autobiography of one of them, Ukawsaw Gronniosaw, which was first published in Bath in about 1770. Gronniosaw was born in about 1710 in what is today northern Nigeria. Although of royal birth he was kidnapped and sold as a slave for two metres of cloth when he was about fifteen. He was a slave in Barbados and America but gained his freedom when his owner died. He later joined the British Army and served in the Caribbean. When he was discharged in the 1760s he came to Britain.

In Britain Gronniosaw took the name James Albert. For a time he lived in London, and he married an English woman who was a weaver. Then the couple moved to Colchester, but both soon became unemployed. Gronniosaw then found work as a builder, but throughout their lives both he and his wife found it difficult to find work and lived in great poverty, constantly in debt.

The family often went without heating and food and at one time lived on four raw carrots for several days. His daughters became ill with smallpox and eventually one died from a fever.

The family were forced to pawn their clothes and sell everything they had to pay their debts and then moved on to Kidderminster.

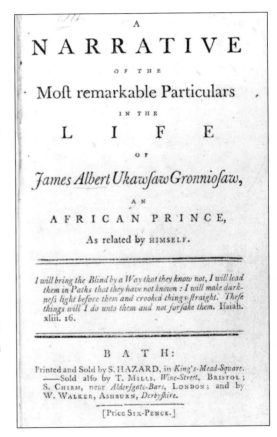

The title page of Gronniosaw's book.

Around 1770 Gronniosaw, with the help of a young woman from Leominster, published the story of his life – *A Narrative of the Most Remarkable Particulars in the Life of James Albert Ukawsaw Gronniosaw, an African Prince.*

Celebrities

Gronniosaw's autobiography is unusual, and at the present time we know little about the lives of other poor Africans in Britain. Written records usually refer to African slaves and servants who became well-known personalities. Francis Barber was brought to England from Jamaica as a slave when he was fifteen years old in about 1750, but was set free when his owner died. For thirty years he was then the servant and companion to the famous writer Dr Samuel Johnson, who paid for him to be educated. After Johnson's death, Barber opened his own school near Lichfield in Staffordshire. The Duchess of Queensbury's servant, Julius Soubise, was known in fashionable society as a swordsman, horseman and musician and was sketched by the artist Thomas Gainsborough.

A portrait of Francis Barber (1735–1801).

CASE study

Ignatius Sancho

Ignatius Sancho was born on a slave ship in 1729 but brought to England at the age of two. He taught himself to read and write and later wrote poetry, two plays, and several musical compositions. He became well known in London amongst writers and artists and his portrait was painted by Gainsborough. Sancho married a Black woman from the Caribbean and they later opened a grocer's shop in Westminster. Sancho became more famous after his death in 1780. A collection of the many letters he had written was published, and immediately became a bestseller. Sancho described himself as 'a coal-black jolly African', but he was concerned about the suffering of African slaves. Even though he spent most of his life in Britain he explained, 'I am only a lodger – and hardly that'. [1]

Ignatius Sancho (1729–1780).

The struggle for freedom

There is evidence that in London Africans got together for their own social events, for weddings, christenings and baptisms. Those Africans who had escaped from their owners and those who were already free soon began to join together to try and improve their conditions in Britain. In 1764 a London newspaper complained that African servants should not be brought into Britain because 'they cease to consider themselves slaves in this free country'. [2]

They also united to help each other escape and to try and end slavery in Britain. In 1773 it was reported in the press that two African men arrested as beggars, were supported and visited 'by upwards of 300 of their countrymen'. [3]

An early nineteenth-century drawing of life in east London.

Slaves and free Africans were helped in their fight against slavery and the slave trade by their supporters in Britain. One of the most famous was Granville Sharp, who took up the fight against slavery in the English law courts. Sharp acted on behalf of runaway slaves who were recaptured by their original owners. He worked with the Black community in London, many of whom attended the court cases. Runaway slaves were also helped by the workers and poor people of London, who were well known for their hatred of slavery.

By the end of the eighteenth century Black people were also taking part in the political events of the capital. In 1780 a Black woman, Charlotte Gardener, was hanged along with others, for her part in the Gordon Riots. Thousands of London's poor had attacked the houses of the wealthy and the Lord Mayor's offices at the Mansion House.

An illustration showing the Gordon Riots of 1780.

3
Fighting slavery in Britain

The main problem affecting most Black people in Britain during the eighteenth century was their status as slaves and the fact that the slave trade continued to grow, with Britain as the main slave trading country. In the seventeenth and early eighteenth centuries African slaves in Britain were regarded by the law as property or goods to be sold, not as human beings. But at the same time English law did not allow human slavery. For a time it was thought that if Africans were baptized or married to English people this would free them from slavery. However, because the slave trade was so valuable to Britain's economy it continued, and Africans brought to Britain by their owners remained slaves.

Many slaves escaped from their owners, so the courts were then asked to judge whether runaways could be recaptured and enslaved in Britain. Finally in 1772, after a long legal battle, Lord Chief Justice Mansfield declared that it was illegal for anyone to forcibly take an African out of the country. He freed James Somerset, a runaway slave who had been recaptured by his owner. Despite this ruling, slavery continued in Britain for another fifty years.

The English abolitionist Granville Sharp defending a Black slave who has been arrested, 1815.

By the 1770s it is clear that London's African population was organizing itself to end slavery and was working closely with Granville Sharp and other leaders of the British abolitionist movement. After the Mansfield judgement 200 Black people met in a public house in Westminster to celebrate Somerset's release. In other areas of the country African slaves were helped to escape by local people, who sometimes even paid for lawyers to fight for their freedom. By this time Britain's Black population may have been as great as 30,000. In London there were large communities in Mile End and Paddington. Black people lived all over the country, especially in the main ports such as Bristol and Liverpool, but also as far afield as Scotland and the Isle of Wight.

Celebrities

Some Black servants and ex-slaves became well known in London, such as Phyllis Wheatley, who became the first Black person to have her writing published in Britain. Phyllis grew up in North America but came to London in 1772. In 1773 her *Poems on Various Subjects* was published, and was later reprinted many times. George Bridgetower became famous as a violinist and composer and was employed by the Prince of Wales, later George IV.

Phyllis Wheatley, c.1753–1785.

As yet, however, we know little about the lives of the majority of Britain's Black population who were servants, labourers, seamen, musicians, shop-keepers and teachers. Two of the most famous Africans were Olaudah Equiano and Kobina Ottobah Cugoano, who became the leaders and spokesmen for London's Black population in the struggle to end the slave trade.

Ottobah Cugoano

Cugoano was born around 1757, in a village on the coast of what is today Ghana, in West Africa. When he was about thirteen he was kidnapped and taken as a slave to Grenada in the Caribbean. In 1772 he was brought to England by his owner and set free. He was advised to get baptized in order not to be sold into slavery again, and took the name John Stuart.

Cugoano soon became involved in the anti-slavery movement and worked with Granville Sharp and other English abolitionists. In 1787 he published a book, possibly written with the help of Equiano, called: *Thoughts and Sentiments on the Evil and Wicked Traffic of the Slavery and Commerce of the Human Species.*

In the book Cugoano describes his capture and transportation to Grenada, but also writes to disprove all the arguments that were then used to justify slavery and the slave trade.

THOUGHTS AND SENTIMENTS

ON THE

EVIL AND WICKED TRAFFIC

OF THE

SLAVERY AND COMMERCE

OF THE

HUMAN SPECIES,

HUMBLY SUBMITTED TO

The INHABITANTS of GREAT-BRITAIN,

BY

OTTOBAH CUGOANO,

A NATIVE of AFRICA.

*He that stealeth a man and selleth him, or maketh merchan-
dize of him, or if he be found in his hand: then that thief
shall die.* LAW OF GOD.

LONDON:

PRINTED IN THE YEAR

M.DCC.LXXXVII.

The title page of Cugoano's book.

He wrote that everyone in England who did not speak out against slavery must be held responsible for it, and he was the first person in England to support the right of slaves to resist and rebel against slavery. Cugoano was the first African to argue for the total abolition of the slave trade by Parliament and for the freeing and compensating of all slaves. Some of Cugoano's proposals, for a British naval patrol of West Africa to stop the slave trade, and for the development of other types of trade between Britain and West Africa, were later adopted by the British Government.

Olaudah Equiano

CASE study

Olaudah Equiano was the most famous African abolitionist in England in the eighteenth century. He was born in 1745 in what is now eastern Nigeria, but when he was eleven both he and his sister were kidnapped, separated from each other and sold as slaves. Equiano was renamed Gustavus Vassa and worked as a slave in Barbados in the Caribbean and in Virginia, North America. He was first brought to England when he was about twelve, but he was twenty-one years old before he managed to buy his freedom. During his life Equiano was a sailor, hairdresser and miner. He travelled widely throughout Europe, America, the Caribbean and even to the Arctic.

Olaudah Equiano (1745–97).

Equiano became one of the leaders of the African community in London, and one of the most well-known personalities in the abolitionist movement. He was also someone who believed that Britain should have a more democratic system of government. In 1789 he wrote an autobiography: *The Interesting Narrative of the Life of Olaudah Equiano, or Gustavus Vassa, the African*. In his book Equiano records from his own experience all the horrors of the slave trade and slavery. The book was extremely popular and Equiano toured Britain and Ireland giving talks to anti-slavery meetings. Equiano, Cugoano and other Africans in London also wrote letters to the press and lobbied Parliament as part of their campaign against slavery.

The Black Loyalists and the Black Poor

In 1784 the Black population of London was increased by the arrival of over 1,000 ex-slaves from North America, who had been promised their freedom for fighting for Britain during the American War of Independence (1775–83). Some of these 'Black Loyalists' had already been free before deciding to fight for Britain, but when they arrived in Britain the government ignored them and only a few were given pensions.

Most were forced to beg on the streets of London. In 1786 some people, including Members of Parliament, argued that the government should introduce a law to stop any more Black people coming to Britain. This was opposed by Black Londoners, who held their own protest meeting in Whitechapel in east London.

Black people worked at all kinds of different trades to try to make a living. This picture from 1792 shows a rabbit seller in London.

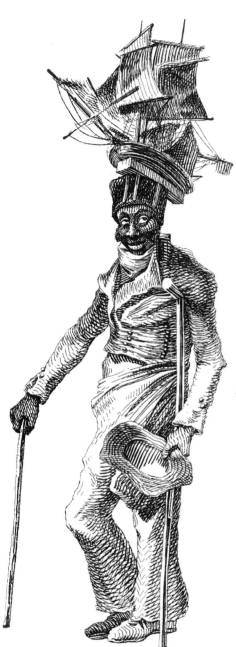

In 1786 a group of wealthy merchants and bankers founded the Committee for the Relief of the Black Poor. They raised funds to provide food, money, clothes and medical help for poor Black people. The Committee soon received financial assistance from the government and launched a plan to transport some of those who had been receiving help to Sierra Leone in West Africa. Indeed, those who did not agree to leave Britain were not given any further help, and some were arrested as vagrants (beggars).

Equiano had been asked by the Committee to take charge of all the provisions for the resettlement scheme. But he soon lost his post for exposing mismanagement, and with Cugoano and many others, publicly opposed the scheme. In 1787 350 Black settlers left for Sierra Leone, many accompanied by their English wives and families, but within four years only sixty were left alive. Many died of disease. The British Government had only been concerned to get rid of a problem and had not properly planned the resettlement scheme.

The abolition of the slave trade

In Britain in the eighteenth century, Africans organized to free themselves from slavery, helped by British sympathizers who supported the fight in the courts. Slaves demanded wages and many then ran away if their owners did not pay them.

From the 1780s onwards the campaign to abolish the slave trade and to free the slaves became one of the largest and most important political movements in Britain's history. Millions of people participated, concerned that slavery and the slave trade affected the rights of everybody in Britain and must be ended. In 1807, Parliament made slave trading illegal for British citizens.

This drawing from 1815 shows Joseph Johnson, a famous beggar and street singer who had been a seaman.

Mary Prince

Although slave trading had been made illegal, slavery was still practised in Britain, as shown by the autobiography of Mary Prince. Mary was born a slave in Bermuda in about 1788. She worked as a servant, children's nurse and salt miner before being brought to Britain by her owners in 1828. Although she was married she was kept as a slave and suffered from continual torture. Once in London, she decided to run away and was helped by the Anti-Slavery Society. In 1831 she wrote *The History of Mary Prince, A West Indian Slave, Related by Herself*. This was the first book written against slavery by a Black woman in Britain and immediately became a bestseller. It played an important role in the campaign to abolish slavery. Finally in 1834, after many years of struggle in Britain and slave revolts in the Caribbean, Parliament declared slavery illegal throughout the British Empire.

CASE *study*

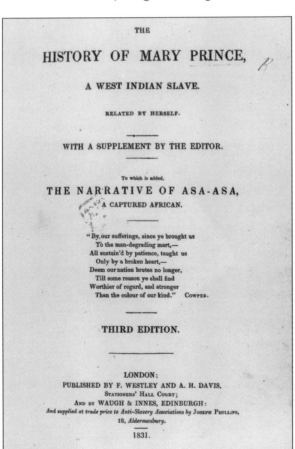

The cover of Mary Prince's book.

4
The 19th-century Black community

By the beginning of the nineteenth century Britain's Black population was scattered throughout the country. There were few Black women, so Black men often married local British women. It is quite likely that many British people have ancestors from Africa and the Caribbean, who have now been forgotten. During the mid-nineteenth century, after the abolition of slavery, fewer Black people entered the country. Those that remained had to cope with all the problems that were the consequence of Britain's industrial revolution. Many country people came to the towns to look for work in the new industries, but there were not always jobs to be found. In the cities, many Black people and other poor people were forced into the workhouse or became beggars. But some jobs were always available. Bill Richmond and Tom Molineux, who both came to Britain from the USA, became famous as bare-knuckle boxers.

A number of other African-Americans visited or stayed in Britain during the nineteenth century. Some were seamen or other workers escaping from slavery in the USA, others were musicians or performers. Some were abolitionists themselves, such as Frederick Douglass and William Wells Brown, who published the first novel by an African-American while he was in London in 1853.

Bill Richmond (1763–1829). Richmond came to Britain as a servant when he was fourteen years old.

Ira Aldridge

Perhaps the best known African-American was Ira Aldridge, the great Shakespearean actor, who came to Britain when he was about eighteen in 1825. He became a British citizen, toured throughout the country and married a woman from Yorkshire. Aldridge had to face the prejudice of London's press, but by the 1850s had established himself on the stage in Britain and in Europe, where he received many awards. He died while on a tour of Poland in 1867.

Ira Aldridge (1804–67) *playing Aaron in Shakespeare's* Titus Andronicus.

CASE study

Soldiers and seamen

As in the past Black people continued to serve in the armed forces. For years army regiments had employed African and Caribbean musicians as military bandsmen. Black men also continued to serve in the Royal Navy, just as Equiano and Gronniosaw had done. As Britain's empire and trade grew, African and Caribbean men were recruited for both the Royal and Merchant Navy. From the mid-nineteenth century some of these seamen from Britain's colonies in the Caribbean and Africa made their homes in Britain's ports. In the East End of London and also in Bristol, Cardiff, Liverpool, and in parts of Scotland, new communities developed made up of these Black seamen and their British wives and families. By 1880 there were many thousands of these seamen working on British ships and living in British ports.

Chelsea pensioners hearing the news of the English victory at the Battle of Waterloo in 1815.

The Black communities in Liverpool

From the late eighteenth century some of the largest Black communities developed in Liverpool. Liverpool became a modern city and a major port as a result of the slave trade, and Africans were regularly sold in auctions there before 1800. Slaves in Liverpool escaped from their owners just as in other parts of the country, and were joined by runaways from other parts of Britain. They found a home in the Toxteth Park area, one of the poorest parts of the city and tried, sometimes without success, to find employment as seamen or in the docks. In the 1840s there was at least one lodging house in Liverpool just for Black seamen, and in the 1860s Charles Dickens wrote of a public house used by Black seamen and workers which was run by a 'jovial Black landlord'. By the end of the nineteenth century many West Africans, especially the Kru seamen from what is now Liberia, had also made their homes in Liverpool.

As in other areas, Liverpool's Black population in the nineteenth century was mainly male. But these men generally married local British women and so a new community developed from the children of these marriages. This pattern has been repeated in Cardiff and some other areas, so that Britain's oldest Black communities have British as well as African and Caribbean ancestors. Sometimes there was opposition to Black and White people marrying each other, and often prejudice against the children of such marriages.

Children in Liverpool in about 1890.

24

Yet in spite of racism and the difficulty of finding work the Black communities in Liverpool and other cities continued to grow throughout the century. It was Liverpool which produced the first British-born Black councillor, alderman and mayor. John Archer was born in Liverpool in 1863 to a Barbadian father and an Irish mother.

John Archer (1863–1932) became mayor of Battersea in south London in 1913.

The Somalis

One group of African seamen who made their homes in Britain during the nineteenth century was from Somalia. Many were Muslims and were joined in Britain by other Muslim seamen, the Yemenis from Aden in the Middle East, which at that time was a British colony. Like other African seamen the Somalis settled in ports such as Liverpool, Cardiff, Hull, east London, and South Shields in Tyneside. They established their own distinct communities, which maintained contact with each other through family and religious ties.

The Butetown mosque in Cardiff. This photograph was taken in 1958.

Religion played an important part in these communities. Muslims in Cardiff and South Shields had the same religious leader in the early part of the twentieth century. Muslims in Cardiff were able to open their own mosque during the 1930s. In 1937 Muslim children in South Shields were allowed to be absent from school during Islamic holidays. The Somalis make up some of the oldest, but least well-known of the African communities in Britain.

Politics

Most Black people were poor and lived amongst the working people in the towns and the countryside. In the nineteenth century workers often lived in terrible conditions, worked long hours and were poorly paid. It was difficult and sometimes illegal for them to form unions and to organize to change their conditions. Until 1918 most were not allowed to vote. Gradually workers did organize themselves to fight for better conditions and wages and for the right to vote. Black people in Britain also played their part in this important political movement. Two of the most famous were William Davidson and William Cuffay.

William Davidson

CASE study

Davidson was born in Jamaica in 1786 and came to Britain when he was fourteen. He joined a group of revolutionaries after the Peterloo Massacre of 1815, in which eleven unarmed demonstrators had been killed by troops. The group was planning an uprising in London, but was encouraged by a police spy also to plan the assassination of the Prime Minister and the Cabinet. This plan became known as the Cato Street Conspiracy. Before it could be carried out, Davidson and the other conspirators were arrested.

They were tried for high treason, found guilty and sentenced to be hanged and beheaded. Davidson and four others were executed in 1820.

The arrest of the Cato Street conspirators.

CASE study

William Cuffay

William Cuffay was born in Kent in 1788 and worked as a tailor. Like many other workers he joined the Chartist movement in the 1830s. The Chartists demanded the vote and other rights for working people. It was the first workers' organization with thousands of members throughout the country. Cuffay became one of the leaders of the London Chartists and was known throughout Britain. In 1848 Cuffay and eleven others were arrested when police spies tried to claim that a rebellion was being planned. At his trial Cuffay pleaded not guilty and courageously defended himself. But he was found guilty and transported to Tasmania for life. Although he was pardoned in 1856, Cuffay remained in Tasmania and continued with his political activities. He died in 1870.

William Cuffay (1788–1870).

Students and Traders

In the nineteenth century Britain's Black communities developed as a result of the influx of seamen and other people from Africa, the Caribbean and North America who came to work. Other important groups were students and merchants both from Africa and the Caribbean. From the eighteenth century African rulers and traders had sent their children, especially sons, to Britain for an education. In the nineteenth century more students from wealthy families came to Britain from the Caribbean. Merchants came to Britain for business reasons, and sometimes set up offices in London or Liverpool.

John Ocansey, who came to Liverpool in 1881 to represent West African traders.

Most of the students came to study law or medicine, but some were trained as teachers or clergymen and some returned home as Christian missionaries. Some of these students remained to practise their professions and then married British women and made their homes in Britain.

Thomas Birch Freeman (1809–90), who was born in Britain, went to West Africa as a Methodist missionary in 1837.

Samuel Coleridge-Taylor

Samuel Coleridge-Taylor was born in London in 1875. His mother was English and his father, a doctor, came from Sierra Leone in West Africa. Coleridge-Taylor was to become one of the most famous classical composers of his day, best known for the choral work *Hiawatha's Wedding Feast*, written in 1898.

He became a professor of composition at Trinity College of Music in London, and toured the USA, where he worked with African-American musicians and composers, and was invited to the White House. Coleridge-Taylor was proud of his African heritage and in many of his compositions used African songs and melodies. He was concerned about the problems facing Black people all over the world and helped to organize the first Pan-African Conference in London in 1900. Tragically, Coleridge-Taylor died in 1912 at the age of thirty-seven.

Samuel Coleridge-Taylor (1875–1912).

Mary Seacole

At present we have very little information on the lives of Black women in Britain in the nineteenth century. Some African and Caribbean women were sent to be educated in Britain, and some African-American women, such as Harriet Jacobs, left accounts of their visits to Britain. But we have few details of the women who were born and grew up as part of Britain's Black population.

CASE study

The most famous Black woman in Britain in the nineteenth century was Mary Seacole, who was born in 1805 and grew up in Jamaica. Her father was Scottish and her mother Jamaican. She travelled at her own expense to the battlefields during the Crimean War (1853–6), and nursed sick and wounded British troops.

Mary Seacole was awarded four medals for her work, but has not become as famous as Florence Nightingale. In 1856 Mary Seacole returned to live in Britain and in 1857 published her autobiography, *The Wonderful Adventures of Mrs Seacole in Many Lands*. She died in London in 1881.

The original cover of Mary Seacole's book.

5
The First World War and the Depression

Black People and the First World War

By the early years of the twentieth century, Britain ruled colonies in the Caribbean as well as in many parts of Africa. Many more people from these areas came to Britain to study and find work and some then remained and settled. People from the Caribbean and Africa came to join the armed forces or the merchant navy and to work in Britain's war industries during the First World War (1914–18). Many people from the Black communities in Britain also enlisted in the services and in munitions work. Several thousand people were brought to Britain from Africa and the Caribbean to do war work, so that British men would be free for military service. By the end of the First World War there may have been about 30,000 Black people in the country.

Troops from the Caribbean serving in France during the First World War, 1916.

Daniel Tull (1888–1918), pictured as a player at Tottenham Hotspur.

Despite problems of discrimination many Black people in Britain did enlist and were later decorated for their bravery. Daniel Tull, who was born in Folkestone in 1888, had been a professional footballer with Tottenham Hotspur. He was made an officer, but was killed in France in 1918.

Some of the communities suffered great wartime losses. Over 1,400 Black seamen from Cardiff lost their lives in the war. Many African and Caribbean troops were also killed. Some of those who were wounded were sent back to Britain for medical treatment and then decided to remain in the country after the war. Black troops, and especially seamen and other workers made a great contribution to the war effort, but after the war many lost their jobs and were not made to feel welcome in Britain.

The 1919 riots

After the First World War many African and Caribbean workers who had been employed in Britain's war industries remained in Britain. Discharged African and Caribbean seamen and soldiers also stayed, so the country's Black population became larger than ever before. Most moved into the Black communities in Liverpool, Cardiff and London or tried to find work in other ports.

Cardiff's Black population, for example, may have been as large as 3,000, Liverpool's over 5,000 and the Black population of London over 20,000 by 1919. But after the war employment was hard to find. Black seamen were discriminated against by trade unions and shipping companies and by the British Government, which attempted to avoid paying them any unemployment benefit.

Racism was on the increase, and the sacrifices of those Black people who had served in the war were forgotten. In 1919 in many of Britain's ports, Black people were attacked and blamed for post-war problems such as unemployment, or for accepting lower wages than White workers, and for being too friendly with White women. Riots and racist attacks occurred in east London, Glasgow, South Shields, Cardiff and other areas. In Liverpool, twenty-four year old Black seaman Charles Wooton was stoned and drowned by a mob of over 200 people. Following several other racist attacks the police were forced to protect over 700 of Liverpool's Black community.

WESTERN MAIL. SATURDAY. JUNE 14. 1919.

RACIAL RIOTS AT CARDIFF.

A cutting from a Cardiff newspaper following the riots against Black people in 1919.

Ernest Marke

Ernest Marke was born in Sierra Leone, West Africa, in 1902. He first came to Britain in 1917 when he was fourteen years old, and has remained in the country throughout most of his long life. In 1975 he published his auto-biography, *Old Man Trouble*, which tells of his experiences in Britain before the Second World War. During the First World War, Ernest Marke stowed away on a ship bound for Britain. The ship was hit by a torpedo from a German submarine, but Ernest was lucky enough to be rescued and brought to England. He then joined another merchant ship which also had to defend itself against a German submarine.

CASE study

Ernest Marke (b.1902), photographed in 1994.

At the age of fifteen Ernest joined the British Army, but within a few months the war ended, and like many Black people in Britain, he found that jobs were now hard to find. Ernest was in Liverpool and found himself in the middle of the 1919 riots. After being attacked and beaten up, Ernest decided to take advantage of a government scheme which offered a free passage and some money to any Black workers who wished to work in what was then the colony of British Guiana, in South America. But no real work was to be found. Ernest returned to sea, but throughout the 1930s he also found work back in Britain as a boxer, gambler, quack (unqualified) doctor, night-club owner and astrologer.

The 1920 and 1930s – Racism and the Colour Bar

The Black communities organized to defend them-selves against attacks in the streets and continued their protests in the courts and in the press. But they were also to face further discrimination. In the 1920s the government introduced two laws which discrim-inated against Black seamen and their families and made it more difficult for them to remain in Britain, find work, or receive unemployment benefit. In Liverpool, Cardiff, London and elsewhere, Black seamen were classed as 'aliens' rather than British subjects. They could be deported and were forced to register with the police, and carry identity cards.

West African seamen aboard the Borrabool *in about 1935.*

During the economic depression of the 1930s, when millions of people were out of work, Black seamen found it increasingly difficult to find work. They and their families often lived in great poverty in Britain's ports. Despite many protests from organizations such as the Coloured Seamen's Union in Cardiff, these laws were still in operation in the 1940s.

Another problem faced by Britain's Black communities in the 1930s was the racism directed against the children of Black men and White women. Some people even argued for laws to prevent Black and White people marrying. Others said that Black seamen should not be allowed to settle in Britain. The

A Christmas party in 1926 organized for the Black community in Canning Town, East London.

children of these marriages were called 'mongrels' and 'half-castes' and all sorts of other names. In some ports, such as Liverpool and Cardiff, they were said to be a major problem, mainly it seems because they were discriminated against and therefore found it hard to get work. Organizations such as the League of Coloured Peoples supported the seamen and their families, and arranged annual outings and parties for Black children.

Unlike the United States or South Africa, Britain has never had laws which have forced Black people to live in separate areas. However in some cities, for many years Black people found it difficult to move out of a particular area, such as Cardiff's Tiger Bay, because of discrimination. In South Shields in the 1930s housing in one area was set aside for Black families. Racism and a colour bar have often prevented Black people from enjoying equal rights with the rest of Britain's population. Until the mid-1960s it was not illegal for Black people to be discriminated against in employment and accommodation and to receive lower wages, or to be refused admission to clubs, hotels and public houses.

Black people in Britain were also concerned about events in Africa. This photograph shows Black workers in Cardiff organizing a protest against the Italian invasion of Ethiopia in 1935.

Black organizations and the press

In order to unite and protest against such treatment, from the 1900s Black people started to form their own social and political organizations, and to publish their own newspapers. Newspapers such as *The Keys*, which was published from 1933 to 1939 by the League of Coloured Peoples, campaigned for an end to racism and the colour bar, and supported those who were struggling for an end to British rule in the colonies.

Some organizations, such as the West African Students Union, founded in London in 1925, were mainly for students. Others were local societies, such as the Cardiff-based Colonial Defence Association, formed around 1927. Some were formed by people of one nationality, such as the British Somali Society, formed in the 1930s. The League of Coloured Peoples, founded in 1931, was concerned to unite everyone of Caribbean and African origin, but also included White members.

African and Caribbean Celebrities in Britain

As in previous centuries, African-Americans, Africans and people from the Caribbean continued to migrate to Britain and often settled amongst the existing Black communities. There were students and businessmen, entertainers, seamen and other workers, as well as those who had been stowaways on boats, hoping to find a job and a better life.

Learie Constantine (Baron Constantine of Maraval and Nelson), 1902–71.

One of those who settled in Britain in the 1920s was the Trinidadian Learie Constantine, a member of the West Indies cricket team, who was later knighted by the Queen and made a life peer. Another was Amy Ashwood Garvey, the first wife of Marcus Garvey. (Marcus Garvey campaigned for Black people to be proud of their African origins.) She opened her own nightclub in London and remained active in Black political organizations until the 1950s. Paul Robeson, the famous African-American singer and actor, also lived in Britain during the 1930s. He became the patron of the West African Students' Union, and the first Black actor since Ira Aldridge to play Othello in London.

During the 1930s London became an important meeting place for African and Caribbean students, writers and political figures. Marcus Garvey and the writer Una Marson, both from Jamaica, lived in Britain during this time. So did the Trinidadians C.L.R. James and George Padmore. Jomo Kenyatta, who later led Kenya to independence from British rule, came to Britain as a student in 1931, and remained in the country until 1946.

Britain's Black population also produced its own personalities. As early as 1886, Arthur Wharton, who was born in Ghana, but grew up in Darlington, became the first man in Britain to run 100 yards (91 metres) in ten seconds. He was also the first Black professional footballer, and played for Sheffield United, Preston North End and Darlington. Len Johnson, born in Manchester in 1902, became one of the most well-known boxers in the country.

Jomo Kenyatta with Sylvia Pankhurst, daughter of the suffragette Emmeline Pankhurst, in 1937.

But Johnson and other Black boxers were barred from competing for any British boxing titles until 1948. In that year Dick Turpin became the first Black man to be allowed to win the British middle-weight championship.

The colour bar made it difficult for Black people to become successful. Hospitals refused to train Black nurses, and even churches discriminated against Black people. This often led to Black people being forced to organize separately.

Boxers Randolph (left) and Dick Turpin, 1949.

In Liverpool in 1931, the Nigerian pastor Daniels Ekarte founded the African Churches Mission, which was a social centre as well as a place for Black people to worship. The African Churches Mission even had its own Scouts and Girl Guides. In Cardiff in 1917 one of the first all-Black cricket teams was formed, the Coloured International Cricket Club. The first plays written by Black writers and with an all-Black cast were performed in London in the 1920s and 1930s.

Some Black people did become successful. One of the most famous was the singer and pianist Leslie 'Hutch' Hutchinson, who originally came from Grenada in the Caribbean. Another famous singer was Evelyn Dove, whose father came from Sierra Leone in West Africa.

Evelyn Dove was born in London in 1902, and became best known for her radio broadcasts during the 1940s, and her television appearances in the 1940s and 1950s. She died aged 85 in 1987.

6
The Second World War and after

During the Second World War many Black people came to Britain to contribute to the war effort. People came for many reasons. As British subjects some felt obliged to come to Britain's aid. Others were strongly opposed to the fascist governments of Italy and Germany, or contributed to the war effort believing this would help the colonies gain greater respect and perhaps some measure of self-government. The African and Caribbean colonies also contributed large sums of money.

There were over 8,000 service men and women from the Caribbean and many skilled technicians who had come to work in the munitions factories. Women volunteers also came from the Caribbean to join the services. Thousands of volunteers from West Africa and the Caribbean arrived to join the Royal Air Force. Even then the government was still reluctant to encourage too many Black people to come to Britain. Those that arrived found that they still had to face the colour bar in the armed forces and might not be allowed into restaurants and hotels. This situation was made worse by the racism of the US forces stationed in Britain, in which Black and White soldiers were still totally segregated.

Volunteer workers from the Caribbean welcomed to London by the Minister of Labour, Ernest Bevin, during the Second World War, July 1942.

The Jamaican writer Una Marson making a wartime Christmas broadcast to the Caribbean for the BBC, December 1943.

Vivian Florent of the Royal Air Force, photographed in 1943.

Many people from Britain's Black communities joined the services or did war work. Some joined the fire brigade and Home Guard or became air-raid wardens. In Liverpool many worked in the munitions factories. Others served in the Merchant Navy or one of the armed forces. From the Florent family in London all four sons joined one of the services. Vivian Florent, who joined the Royal Air Force, was killed in action aged twenty-three. In total, over 200,000 people from Britain's colonies lost their lives in the war.

Even during the war Black people continued to suffer discrimination. In 1943 Amelia King, a young Black woman from Stepney in east London, was rejected by the Women's Land Army in Essex, after local people refused to employ or accommodate her. The most famous case was that of the cricketer, Learie Constantine, who was employed by the government during the war. He was refused entry to a hotel in London in 1943. Constantine took the hotel to court and won his case, but many other Black people were not so fortunate, and complained of racism in the forces and munitions factories.

Black firemen aboard a steamer in Cardiff during the Second World War.

After the war

At the end of the war in 1945 a Labour Government was elected in Britain. Black people in Britain, and especially in the colonies, looked forward to greater opportunities and the possibility of an end to colonial rule. A number of new Black organizations had been formed in Britain during the war, and Negro Welfare Centres were established by Africans in Liverpool, Manchester and Hull to look after the growing Black communities in these cities. In October 1945, Black organizations in Britain held the fifth Pan-African Congress, in Manchester. It was attended by representatives from organizations in Africa, the Caribbean and the USA. The Congress called for self-government in the colonies, and demanded an end to the colour bar in Britain. Many of those attending, such as Kwame Nkrumah and Jomo Kenyatta, later became the leaders of independent African countries.

The Pan-African Congress in Manchester, 1945. Here, one of the organizers, Dr Peter Milliard, addresses the conference. On his left are Amy Ashwood Garvey, the Mayor of Manchester, and I.T.A. Wallace-Johnson, a trade union organizer from Sierra Leone.

Thousands of workers came from the Caribbean and Africa to help rebuild Britain after the war.

Many of those from Africa and the Caribbean remained in Britain after the war. But just as after the First World War, those who had contributed to the war effort were not always welcomed. In 1948 in Liverpool there were attacks on the Black community. Many people were injured or arrested after the Seamen's Union tried to bar Black seamen from working in British ports.

Immigration

During the late 1940s and 1950s the British Government encouraged more immigrants from the colonies in the Caribbean, Africa and elsewhere. After the war, in which many had lost their lives, there was a shortage of workers and a need to rebuild Britain. London Transport recruited workers from Barbados, Trinidad and Jamaica, and the National Health Service recruited nurses in the Caribbean and West Africa. Many more students from these areas also came to Britain after the war.

Black and White people worked together in British factories, as shown by this photograph from 1955.

The colour bar made it very hard for new migrants to find accommodation.

The new migrants often settled in the older Black communities, or created new communities in cities like Birmingham, Nottingham and Leeds. Between 1945 and 1958 over 125,000 people from the Caribbean came to settle in Britain. As a result Britain's Black population greatly increased in size. In 1991 there were nearly 1 million Black people in Britain, over half of them British born.

Caribbean and African migrants faced many difficulties in Britain. The colour bar made it difficult to find accommodation. Immigrant workers were not always welcomed into trade unions and were often paid lower wages than White workers.

In 1958, large-scale attacks on Black people occurred in Notting Hill in west London and in Nottingham. Once again, organizations were formed to fight against racism. In 1962 the Conservative Government introduced the first of a series of Immigration Acts to limit the number of African, Caribbean and Asian immigrants arriving in Britain.

Both adults and children dress up in spectacular costumes for Leeds carnival, a Caribbean festival that takes place every summer.

Since 1973 immigration to Britain from the Caribbean and Africa has largely been halted, apart from those who have entered the country as refugees from countries such as Somalia and Ethiopia. Most of the country's Black population are now born and grow up in Britain, but may still retain their links with Africa and the Caribbean. In this way the culture of the Black communities and of Africa and the Caribbean have become a part of British culture. Many people are now familiar with African and especially Caribbean food, such as yam and plaintain, and with cultural events such as Notting Hill and other carnivals. The music of the Caribbean such as reggae and soca is very popular. Today in Britain's main cities it is often African and Caribbean churchgoers and churches who are giving new life to the country's Christian traditions.

In many areas of life from sport to politics Black people in Britain, despite many difficulties, are continuing to make their contributions. As this book has shown, people of African and Caribbean origin have been an important part of Britain's population for many centuries.

Glossary

Abolitionists Those who campaigned for an end to the slave trade.

Anti-Slavery Society A society formed in 1823 in Britain to campaign for an end to slavery.

Cabinet The cabinet is made up of the most important members of the government.

Chartist Movement The first national political movement of the working class in Britain. Established in the 1830s it took its name from a six-point charter published in 1838, which amongst other things demanded the vote for all adult males.

Colour Bar Barring Black people from jobs, accommodation and public places because of the colour of their skin.

Crimean War A war fought largely by Britain and France against Russia from 1853–6.

Expulsion Forcing someone to leave a place or country.

Home Guard Part-time volunteers organized to defend Britain from attack during the Second World War. It was later made famous by the television comedy *Dad's Army*.

Industrial Revolution The growth of modern factories and transport systems which occurred in Britain from around 1750.

Oral history Spoken rather than written history which can often provide an eye-witness account of past events.

Pan-African Has come to mean anything concerned not just with Africa or those from the African continent, but with all those of African origin in the Caribbean, the Americas and throughout the world.

Revolutionaries Those who organize to overthrow the existing political system.

Segregation Forcing Black people to use separate and usually worse facilities than White people.

Finding out more

There are now a number of publications available on the history of Black people in Britain. Those which offer a general introduction for secondary readers include:

Black and British by David Bygott (Oxford, 1992)

Black Settlers in Britain 1555–1958 by Nigel File and Chris Power (Heinemann,1988)

The Fight Against Racism: A Pictorial History of Africans and Asians in Britain (Institute of Race Relations, 1986) Useful pictorial material from the post-war period.

Many autobiographies, biographies and oral histories are now also available and are suitable for secondary readers. These include:

Highfield Rangers: An Oral History (Leicester Living History Unit, 1993)

The History of Mary Prince, a West Indian Slave edited by Moira Ferguson (Pandora, 1987)

In Troubled Waters – Memoirs of Seventy Years in England by Ernest Marke (Karia, 1986)

The Life of Olaudah Equiano edited and abridged by Paul Edwards (Longman, 1989)

The Motherland Calls – African-Caribbean Experiences and *'Sorry No Vacancies': Life Stories of Senior Citizens from the Caribbean* (Notting Dale Urban Studies Centre and Ethnic Communities Oral History Project, 1992)

The Somali Sailors by Similola Coker (Ethnic Communities Oral History Project, 1992)

The Sun Shone on our Side of the Street: Aunt Esther's Story by Stephen Bourne and Esther Bruce (Ethnic Communities Oral History Project, 1991)

The Tiger Bay Story by Neil Sinclair (Butetown History and Arts Project, 1993) One of a series of *Life Stories from Tiger Bay* published by Butetown History and Arts Project.

The Wonderful Adventures of Mrs Seacole in Many Lands by Mary Seacole, introduction by Ziggi Alexander (Falling Walls Press, 1984)

Further information for teachers

General

Africans in Britain edited by David Killingray (Frank Cass, 1994)

Black Britannia – A History of Blacks in Britain by Edward Scobie (Johnson Publishing Company, 1972)

The Black Celts – An Ancient African Civilization in Ireland and Britain by Ahmed Ali and Ibrahim Ali (Punite Publications, 1992)

Black Music in Britain: Essays in Afro-Asian Contributions to Popular Music edited by Paul Oliver (Open University Press, 1990)

Black People in Britain by Folarin Shyllon (Oxford University Press, 1977)

Black Personalities in the Era of the Slave Trade edited by James Walvin and Paul Edwards (Macmillan, 1983)

Black and White in Colour: Black People in British Television since 1936 edited by Jim Pines (British Film Institute, 1992)

Black Writers in Britain 1760–1890 edited by Paul Edwards and David Dabydeen (Edinburgh University Press, 1991)

Britain Since 1930 – Immigration and the Black Presence in Britain (Teachers Resource Centre for Multicultural Education, Leicester, 1994)

Essays on the History of Blacks in Britain edited by J. S. Gundara & I. Duffield (Avebury, 1992)

Hogarth's Blacks by David Dabydeen (Manchester University Press, 1987)

The Horrors of Slavery and other writings by Robert Wedderburn, edited by Iain McCalman (Edinburgh University Press, 1992)

The Letters of Ignatius Sancho edited by Paul Edwards and Polly Rewt (Edinburgh University Press, 1994)

The Making of the Black Working Class in Britain by Ron Ramdin (Gower, 1987)

Many Struggles: West Indian Workers and Service Personnel in Britain 1939–45 by Marika Sherwood (Karia Press, 1985

Nature Knows No Colour-Line by J.A. Rogers (H.M. Rogers, 1980)

Presence and Prestige: Africans in Europe by H.W. Debrunner (Basel Africa Bibliography, 1979)

Staying Power – The History of Black People in Britain by Peter Fryer (Pluto, 1984)

Under the Imperial Carpet: Essays in Black History 1780–1950 edited by R. Lotz and I. Pegg (Rabbit Press, 1986)

The 1945 Manchester Pan-African Congress Revisited by H. Adi and M. Sherwood (New Beacon Books, 1995)

Local History

Black People in Warwickshire's Past (Educational Development Services, Warwickshire, 1994)

The Black Presence in Nottingham (Castle Museum and ACFF Nottingham, 1993)

Caribbeans in Wandsworth by Gloria Lock (Wandsworth Borough Council, 1992)

Daniels Ekarte and the African Churches Mission by Marika Sherwood (Savannah Press, 1994)

Never Counted Out – The Story of Len Johnson, Manchester's Black Boxing Hero and Communist by Michael Herbert (Dropped Aitches Press, 1992)

The Peopling of London – Fifteen Thousand Years of Settlement from Overseas edited by Nick Merriman (Museum of London, 1993) Includes chapters: 'Africans and Caribbeans in London' by Peter Fraser, and 'Somalis in London' by Shamis Hussein.

Staying Power by Marij van Helmond and Donna Palmer (National Museums and Galleries on Merseyside, Liverpool, 1991)

Videos/slides

Caribbean Women in World War II: Four Black Women's Oral History of Wartime Service (Caribbean Ex-Service Women's Association and the London Borough of Hammersmith and Fulham)

Out of the Shadows, An Audio-Visual History of the Black Presence in Britain 1500–1950 (Catholic Association for Racial Justice)

Useful addresses

Association for the Study of African, Caribbean and Asian Culture and History in Britain, c/o ICS, 28 Russell Square, London WC1B 5DS

Bedfordshire Record Office Equal Opportunities Project, County Hall, Bedford, MK42 9AP

Birmingham Black Oral History Project, 70 Villa Rd, Handsworth, Birmingham B19 1NH

Black Cultural Archives, 378 Coldharbour Lane, London SW9 8LF

Butetown History and Arts Project, 5 Dock Chambers, 55 Bute St, Cardiff CF1 6AH

Ethnic Communities Oral History Project, 2 Royal Parade, Dawes Rd, London SW6 7RE

Ipswich African Caribbean Oral History Project c/o Suffolk Record Office, Gateacre Rd, Ipswich IP1 2LG

Northamptonshire Black History Group, c/o Wellingborough Racial Equality Council, Victoria Centre, Palk Rd, Wellingborough NN8 1HT

Notting Dale Urban Studies Centre, 189 Freston Rd, London W10 6TH

Oldham Local Studies Library, 84 Union St, Oldham OL1 1DN

The Peopling of London Project, Museum of London, 150 London Wall, London EC2Y 5HN

Research

In addition to reading, why not conduct your own research? You could record the oral histories of relatives or neighbours, especially those with long and interesting lives.

Many libraries and museums now have useful information about local Black history. If there seems to be no local information contact your local library, museum or history society and ask them to start looking.

Index

Numbers in **bold** indicate subjects that are shown in pictures as well as in the text.